Burnout REimagined

Why You're Not Burned Out —You're Overflowing (and What to Do About It)

Carol L Rickard, LCSW

WellYOUniversity® Publications

Contents

Burnout REimagined

by Carol L Rickard, LCSW

ISBN: 978-1-947745-62-9 (paperback)
ISBN: 978-1-947745-63-6 (Ebook)

WellYOUniversity® Publications

A Division of Well YOUniversity, LLC
5 Zion Rd.
Hopewell, NJ 08525
609.462.7643
www.StressSMARTER.zone
Carol@StressSmarter.zone

About This Book

I doubt you have read a  like this!

I like to use a lot of pictures, 

analogies, & word art which help

information *stick* in the brain!

I call my approach:

SMARTheory™

(It's what makes my books and trainings

different from all others!)

KNOWLEDGE

is the *left brain* at work.

This is where YOU ***know*** what to do!

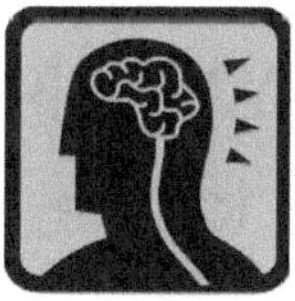

Since I use “pictures” & “images”, I end up

tapping into the other side of the brain –

the right side!

With both sides working

on the same page,

the result is getting people to

Move knowledge into ACTION!

This book is designed to be more like

“a workshop in a book”

So, you walk away with tools & strategies

you can begin to use immediately!

Each chapter includes:

Overflow Insight —

The *single* most important **takeaway** from each chapter.

Try This —

A short *practical* exercise you can **do immediately.** Not someday. Right now.

Chapter Takeaway —

One sentence that **captures** everything. Because the best ideas should

What This Book Is — And Is Not

This book is **NOT** about

eliminating stress.

That's not realistic —

especially for the kind of person

who's drawn to *high-performing,*

high-stakes, **deeply meaningful** work.

This book is about what happens AFTER

STRESS is activated.

Do you stay in it?

Or do you ***complete it?***

That **?** changes everything.

And is the one this book

is **designed** to answer.

A Quick Road Map

Here's what each part of this book will introduce you to:

Introduction: The Day I Almost Lost Everything

Before we dive into the system, I want to share the personal story that started all of this. Three weeks of migraines. A doctor's office. A bottle of root beer in a car. And the discovery that changed my life — and has since changed the lives of thousands of professionals just like you.

Part 1: The Reframe

Chapters 1-3

Everything you think you know about burnout is about to change. Here you'll discover the core insight behind the **Overflow RESET System™** — why you are not burned out but overflowing — and meet the simple metaphor that makes everything instantly clear. The tub. The faucet. The drain.

Part 2: RESET — Turn Off the Faucet

Chapters 4-5

Before you can release stress, you must stop it from escalating. You'll learn why stress never really goes away on its own — and the simple 10-second tool that sends your nervous system one clear signal. The threat is gone. Stand down.

Part 3: RELEASE — Open the Drain

Chapters 6-8

This is the step most stress programs completely miss. You'll learn why managing stress is only half the job — and discover a complete toolkit of release tools you can use anytime, anywhere, that nobody even has to know you are doing.

Part 4: PROTECT — Keep the Tub From Overflowing

Chapters 9-11

Even if you reset and release during the day — something can undo all of it. What happens after your day ends. You'll learn how to stop carrying work home with you, create a powerful end-of-day ritual and protect yourself with the same commitment you give to everyone else.

Part 5: The Complete System

Chapter 12 + Conclusion

In the final section we bring everything together into one complete picture — and I share the truth that has driven everything I do. Your passion for your work does not have to destroy you. It can actually sustain you. When you have the right system.

"You are not burned out. You are overflowing. And now — we fix that."

One Last Thing Before You Begin

You *picked* up this book for a reason.

Maybe…

- You're *exhausted.*
- You're *running on empty.*
- You love what you do but you're starting to have the thought:

'I can't keep doing this.'

Whatever brought you here —

I am glad you are here.

What I'm about to share with you

IS NOT **THEORY**.

It ***IS NOT*** generic wellness advice.

IT IS a real system built on

34 years of clinical experience —

that works in *real time,*

in the middle of your actual life.

You're about to **discover** something

most people *spend*

their entire careers never finding:

That the answer's never about doing less.

It's about *learning* how to **RELEASE!**

Let's begin.

— **Carol Rickard, LCSW**
2x TEDx Speaker | Healthcare Burnout Expert
Creator of the Overflow RESET System™

This Book Is For You

3 weeks in a row I left my dream job

early with a **migraine** so *crushing*

I thought my head would explode.

I was a *clinical social worker* teaching

STRESS management at a hospital.

But I was *falling*

APART.

My doctor finally asked:

"Carol — what's got you so stressed out?"

The **confusing** part was…

I was DOING everything right.

And none of it was working.

It wasn't until I *knocked* over the bottle of root beer in my car that **EVERYTHING** clicked.

I *watched* the pressure build inside that bottle and thought…

'This is exactly what life has been doing to me.'

What I THOUGHT was **BURNOUT**

Was actually

BUILT UP STRESS

That realization became

the **Overflow RESET System™**.

And it CHANGED everything.

This  will **CHANGE**

your life if you WILL use

what you're about to **discover!**

You're exactly who this

was *written* for. 

— Carol

Let's move on! ⇨

PART 1:
THE REFRAME

Chapter 1:
You're Not Burned Out

I'm so ***glad*** you're here.

And I want to TELL you something

before we go any further…

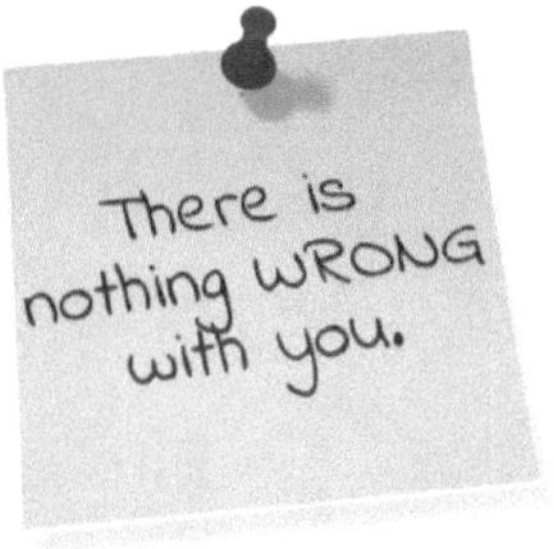

You are *not* broken.

You are *not* burned out.

Something else is happening.

And once I ***show you*** what it is —

— everything will make more sense.

Maybe you're a...

Nurse

First responder

Paramedic

Social worker

Law enforcement officer

Teacher

Therapist

Executive

Firefighter

Caregiver

The job titles are different. But you have *something* **profound** in common.

You CHOSE a life of showing up for other people. *Day after day.*

In some of the most **demanding** situations.

You ♡ **what** you DO.

But something has *shifted.*

And you're *starting* to **wonder** —

'How much longer can I keep doing this?

OVERFLOW INSIGHT:
You're not failing. You're full. And there's a critical difference between those two things.

Here's what I've seen over **34** years of working with people in **high-responsibility** roles.

They THINK it's 

BUT it's not.

They're just carrying more **than** the **human system** was designed for

WITHOUT ever being **taught** *how to* **release it.**

That's not a **personal** failure.

That's a GAP in your *training.*

TRY THIS:

Finish this sentence honestly:

"Lately I have been feeling ____________________."

Write whatever comes.
Do not overthink it. Just let it out.

Because naming it is the very first step.

CHAPTER TAKEAWAY:

*What you are feeling is not burnout.
It is something far more specific —
and far more solvable.*

Chapter 2:
Your Superpower Has a Limit

Whether you *realize it* or ***not***...

Your training has taught you to do

Something incredible.

You *learned* to **compartmentalize.**

Some Examples:

A firefighter walks into a burning building while everyone else runs out. They don't fall apart. They stay focused. They do the job.

A first responder arrives at an accident scene and sees things no human being should have to see. They do not freeze. They act.

A social worker sits with a family in crisis — absorbing their pain, their fear, their chaos — and stays calm enough to help.

A nurse loses a patient they have cared for all week and twenty minutes later must walk into the next room and be fully present for someone else.

How do they do that?

They *put it* in a **compartment.**

They FILE it away.

They ***keep going.***

OVERFLOW INSIGHT:
That ability to compartmentalize? It's your superpower. It's what makes people in your profession extraordinary.

But *here's* what **NOBODY**

told you in training...

Those **compartments** have a *limit.*

- Every difficult shift.
- Every traumatic scene.
- Every impossible decision.
- Every person you could not save.
- Every time you absorbed someone else's pain so they did not have to carry it alone.

Every time you *compartmentalize…*

something ***gets stored.***

NOT
processed.

NOT
released

STORED

And if you **NEVER** *learned*

how to release what goes in —

Eventually it **OVERFLOWS**

TRY THIS:

Ask yourself honestly:

"What has been going into my compartment lately?"

Make a quick list. Don't overthink it. Just write down everything that has been filling your space — at work AND at home.

Because you cannot drain what you cannot see.

🗝 CHAPTER TAKEAWAY:

Compartmentalization is your greatest professional strength. But without a way to release what goes in — it becomes the very thing that brings you down.

Chapter 3:
Meet Your Tub

Imagine you're *this* tub.

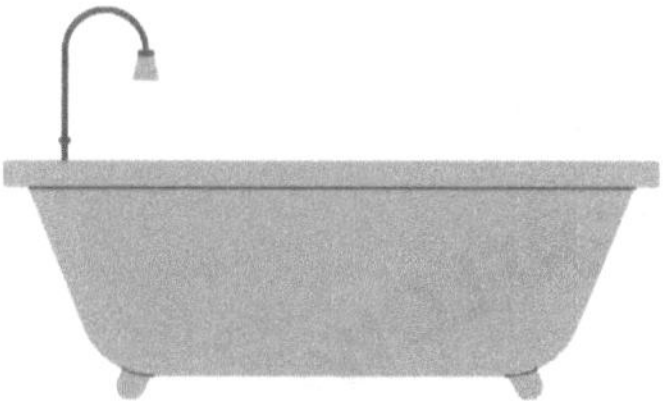

Every *stressful* moment in your day is

water coming from the  into the tub.

- A *traumatic* call… ***water***
- An *overwhelming* caseload… ***more water***
- A *loss* you couldn't prevent… ***water***
- *Paperwork* at the end of the day… ***water***
- Driving home & *replaying it* all in your head… ***still more water***

Now —

What *happens*...

if **the faucet** keeps *running*

& the drain ***stays closed?*** 

The tub **OVERFLOWS**

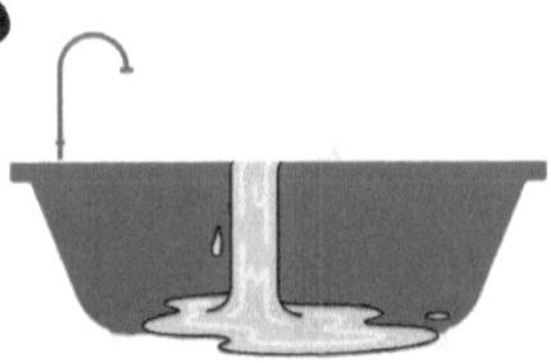

And THAT'S what you've been feeling.

- The ***exhaustion.***
- The ***overwhelm.***
- The ***irritability.***
- The feeling - ***I can't do this anymore.***

It's **not** that you are weak.

It's **not** that you can't do this work.

It's **not** BURNOUT…

It's your tub OVERFOWING!

Because…

No one ever **TAUGHT** you *how* to ***open the drain.***

💡 **OVERFLOW INSIGHT:**
Overflowing tubs do not need to be replaced. They need to be drained. And that changes everything.

Here's the most **IMPORTANT** thing I

want you to **take** *away…*

BURNOUT sounds permanent…

It's like **something** is *gone* —

your passion, your strength,

your ability to keep going.

But overflow? *It has a SOLUTION!*

You **need** to do **2** simple steps.

1) ***TURN OFF*** the faucet 

2) ***OPEN*** the drain. 

That's the entire **Overflow RESET System™**

And it only takes seconds to complete!

And in the next chapters

I'll ***show* you** exactly to

how to do BOTH STEPS —

TRY THIS:

On a scale of 1-10 — how full is
your tub right now?

1 = barely any water
10 = overflowing

Write your number down.

Now ask yourself —
when did it start feeling this full?

That awareness is the
beginning of everything.

CHAPTER TAKEAWAY:

You are not burned out. Your tub is overflowing. And an overflowing tub has a solution — turn off the faucet and open the drain.

PART 2:

RESET –
Turn Off The Faucet

Chapter 4:
Why Stress Never Really Goes Away

I want to ask you a 

When a stressful situation *ENDS* —

does the stress ***end with it?***

STRESS is not *a feeling.*

It's a biological process.

When something stressful *happens…*

your body **responds** *instantly.*

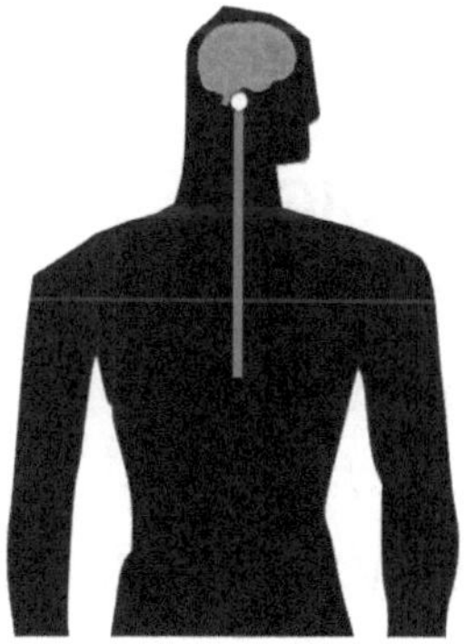

Our Brain
sends signals
& *energy to*

↓

Our Body
We can't stop this –
Only MANAGE IT!

Stress is a <u>loop</u> that ***MUST*** be completed.

There are 3 stages:

Beginning	⇨	Response ***TRIGGERED***
Middle	⇨	Response ***ACTIVE***
End	⇨	Response ***COMPLETED***

And here's what nobody talks about…

That loop **MUST** be

physically completed to end.

💡 OVERFLOW INSIGHT:

We've been taught to manage the stressors in our lives.
But we've forgotten how to complete the stress cycle itself.

Let me explain what I mean...

Picture this antelope on

the *African Savanna.*

Now picture this leopard

with *its grip on it.*

The antelope's stress response **kicks in!**

Every system is activated instantly.

- ✓ *Heart racing.*
- ✓ *Muscles firing.*
- ✓ *Survival energy at its absolute peak.*

The leopard gets *distracted* and RUNS OFF

Here's what happens next...

The antelope doesn't just *shake it off*

and go back to grazing.

First,

it takes a *few* ***S l o w*** breaths.

Then,

Its ENTIRE body **trembles** — literally

shakes — for about 30 seconds.

And *THEN…*

It goes back to grazing like

nothing happened!

That shaking? That's the ***physical completion*** of the *stress response cycle.*

A CLEAR signal — the

threat is *gone*, it's SAFE! to *stand down.*

And the ***CYCLE CLOSED.***

> ***"The cycle has to be completed.***
>
> ***Not managed. Completed."***

IMPORTANT:

We **humans** are the ONLY SPECIES

who *keeps* the leopard <u>alive</u> <u>inside</u>

l o n g after it is gone….

The difficult situation ends — but the stress

stays in your body. 

The crisis is over — but your nervous

system **is still activated.**

You drive home — but your mind is still **running the day on repeat.**

You think because the situation ENDED the **STRESS** ended with it.

But the cycle is still running. 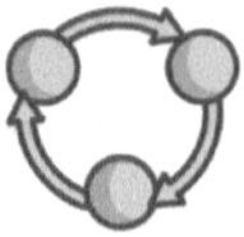

Waiting to be completed.

Here's what it should  like:

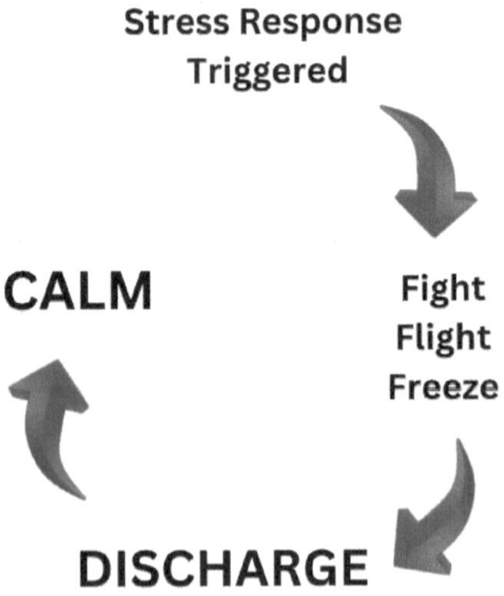

Let me give you some specific examples of how this shows up in life:

A firefighter responds to a horrific scene. Adrenaline fires. Every sense heightens. The body does exactly what it is supposed to do. The scene clears.

The crew heads back to the station.

But an hour later that firefighter is snapping at a colleague over something small. Cannot eat. Feels simultaneously wired and exhausted.

That's not weakness.

It's an incomplete stress cycle still running.

A nurse loses a patient they have cared for all week. Twenty minutes later they must walk into the next room and be fully present for someone else.

They do it. Because that is what they do.

But the tension in their shoulders never left. The heaviness? Still there.

That's not burnout.

That's a biological loop that never got closed.

💡 **OVERFLOW INSIGHT:**

Every stressor that never gets completed is still running. That's why the tub keeps filling even on your days off.

TRY THIS:

Think about your last really stressful day at work.

Ask yourself honestly:

"Did I actually release that stress — or did I just move on from it?"

If the answer is move on — you're not alone. Most people never learned there was another option.

But now you do.

CHAPTER TAKEAWAY:

Stress is a biological loop that must be physically completed. When it is not — it keeps running. That's what fills your tub.

Chapter 5:
Turn Off the Faucet

So how do you ***complete the cycle?***

How do you

Turn off the faucet?

You *send* your nervous system a

biological signal that the

threat is ***gone.*** You're

And the ***FASTEST WAY*** to do that?

Your BREATH.

Just *intentional* breathing.

OVERFLOW INSIGHT:
Your breath is the one tool you always have with you. Nobody can see you using it. And it works in 10 seconds.

The *RESET Breath* is all you do:

Breathe IN:

(thru the nose)

S L O W
count of 5

Breathe OUT:

(thru the mouth)

S L O W
count of 5

Do That 3 Times

That's it!

10 seconds. *Anywhere. Anytime.*

- ✓ Before a difficult conversation.
- ✓ In your car before a shift.
- ✓ Between patients or meetings.
- ✓ Before you walk through your front door at the end of the day.

"In 2-3-4-5. Out 2-3-4-5. Three times. Faucet off."

Here's what's happening when you do it.

When we SLOW DOWN our breathing,

Our 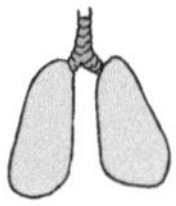 ***signal our heart*** to **slow down.**

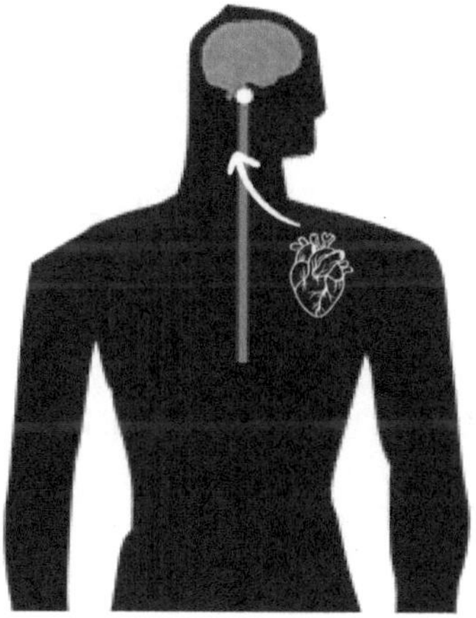

Our heart then ***signals our brain*** to

turn off the stress faucet!

In seconds you shift *from* **fight or flight** —

straight back toward BALANCE.

You'll feel it as…

Your shoulders *dropping slightly.*
A *deeper breath.*
A small *moment of quiet.*

That's your **NERVOUS SYSTEM**

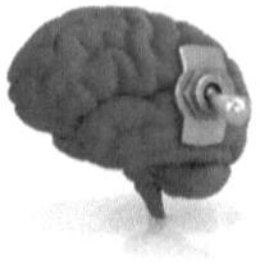

receiving the signal.

Threat is gone. *Stand down.*

That is the faucet turning off.

You turned

off the faucet.

TRY THIS:

Do it right now. Seriously —
put the book down and try it.

Breathe in through your nose —
1, 2, 3, 4, 5.
Breathe out through your mouth —
1, 2, 3, 4, 5.

Do that three times.

Now check in with your body.

Do you feel that slight settling?
That tiny release in your shoulders?
That moment where your brain went quiet
for just a second?

That's your nervous system resetting.

That is the faucet turning off.

One Important Thing

RESET Breathing *turns off* the 

It **DOES NOT** **drain the tub.**

The <u>pressure</u> that's already ***BUILT UP?***

It's still there.

That's why so many people say —

*I tried breathing & it **helps***

but it doesn't last.

They're not doing anything wrong…

Just **MISSING** the **2nd Step!**

Step #1 – **RESET**

Step #2 - **RELEASE**

Both **steps**

Done together in <u>order</u> —

That's HOW the **CYCLE**

COMPLETES

And that's *exactly*

what we look at next:

Step #2 - How to RELEASE

🔑 CHAPTER TAKEAWAY:

RESET breathing sends your nervous system one clear signal — the threat is gone, you are safe. Ten seconds. Anywhere. But it is only the first step.

PART 3:

RELEASE –
Open The Drain

Chapter 6: Why Managing Is Not Enough

Here's the step **most**

stress programs completely *miss.*

It's also why people do all the right things:

- *Exercise*
- *Meditation*
- *Deep breathing*

AND **still** feel **overwhelmed.**

They're 

the stress.

But they're NOT **releasing it.**

There's a **critical** difference

between those 2 things.

Managing = **TURN OFF** 

It will 

the level from **RISING**

But the water <u>already</u> in the tub?

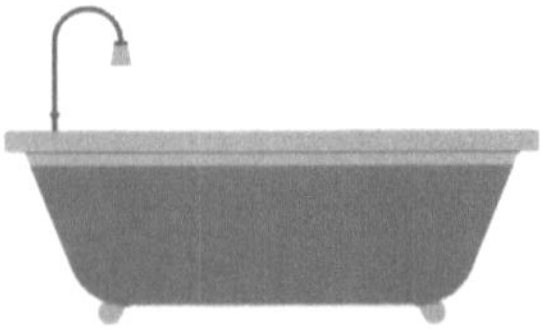

It's still there.

> **OVERFLOW INSIGHT:**
> *You CAN'T think your way out of stress.*
> *It lives in your body.*
> *And that means releasing it*
> *requires a physical response.*

Remember our  ?

After the leopard left it DIDN'T just

take a breath and go back to *grazing.*

It shook. Its entire body **trembled**

for about 30 seconds.

That shaking wasn't weakness.

That's its ***nervous system*** doing

something *extraordinarily* intelligent —

physically discharging survival energy

that had BUILT UP during the threat.

THEN the cycle was complete.

It's IMPORTANT you to ***understand*** this:

Stress ISN'T just *emotional.*

It's **physical.** ⟹ It *lives* in your body.

This means you CAN'T:

➔ Logic your way through it.

➔ Tell yourself to calm down.

➔ Just breathe & hope it goes away.

Your body needs to:

Move

Express

Discharge

all the ENERGY building up

day after day.

"You can't drain the tub if you never open the drain."

Exercise is one of the most *powerful* **release tools** we have.

When you go for *a run*, take *a walk, hit the gym* — your body's doing exactly what the antelope did. ***Moving that stress energy*** OUT of your system.

But here's the reality:

- You CAN'T always *go for a run*.
- You CAN'T do *jumping jacks* in the middle of a shift.

- You CAN'T *take a long walk* when the next situation is already waiting.

More importantly:

Physical movement DOESN'T release the

emotional stress that people carry.

You're NOT just holding physical energy.

It's grief. Frustration. Guilt.

That needs an **emotional release** too.

That's *exactly* what the

next chapter is about.

TRY THIS:

Ask yourself honestly:

"When I have a hard day — do I actually release it? Or do I just push through and move on?"

If the answer is push through — notice how that has been working for you.

Because the tub does not empty itself.

CHAPTER TAKEAWAY:

Managing stress turns off the faucet. Releasing stress opens the drain. You need both. And most people have only ever been taught one.

Chapter 7:
Open the Drain

32 years ago, I was working in a ***women's trauma*** program.

One of the techniques we used was something SIMPLE but extraordinarily **powerful:**

1. *Write it* down.
2. **Do not** read it.
3. DESTROY it immediately.

I called it **Dump N Destroy.**

It's a tool I've been using and teaching ever since.

I have **never** seen a *simpler* tool

create such an immediate and

profound sense of relief.

Here is WHY it works…

💡 **OVERFLOW INSIGHT:**
Writing releases the pressure. Reading reloads it. The moment you destroy what you wrote — your brain registers: this thing I was holding, I am now letting go.

Dump N Destroy vs Journaling

When you journal you *write* — and then

you ***read it back***. You reflect.

You analyze. You process.

That's a valuable practice.

But it **keeps you** IN YOUR HEAD.

You're re-examining. You're reliving.

Dump N Destroy is the *opposite.*

You write to GET IT OUT.

➔ ***Not*** to examine it.

➔ ***Not*** to understand it.

Just to **get it out** of your body &

put it somewhere *outside of you.*

And then — and this is the critical part —

DESTROY IT.

Immediately. Without reading it.

- ✓ You crumple it up.
- ✓ You rip it apart.
- ✓ You throw it away.

When you write **by hand** & then

physically discard what you wrote —

your brain registers something **PROFOUND:**

This thing I was holding —
I'm now letting go.

This is not just psychological.

It's **neurological.**

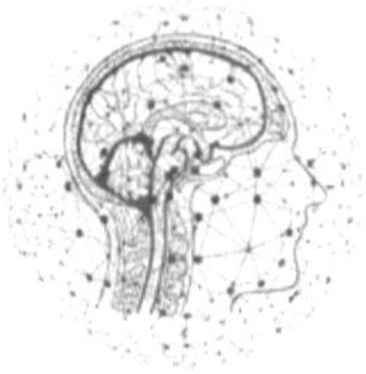

The act of *physical destruction* SENDS a

completion signal to your nervous system.

The cycle closes.

Three Ways to Do It

Option 1: Classic Dump N Destroy

1. Grab paper.
2. Write whatever's on your mind & in your body. Don't censor it!
3. Do not read it.
4. Crumple it up. Throw it away.

Option 2: Crayon Scribble

Sometimes you're ***not*** sure what you feel. You just ***feel full.***

This is where crayons are the BEST choice. Because you *don't have to know* what you're **thinking** or ***feeling!***

Go buy yourself a 

Pick the **color** that

matches how you **feel.**

And *scribble.* **No words**. No sentences.

No coherent thought required.

BONUS TIP:

Release the intensity

of your *feelings*

by pushing harder on the paper!

☑ Then crumple it up.

☑ Throw it away.

☑ And feel lighter.

Option 3: The Magic Palm Dump

No paper. *No* crayons.

Nothing but your hand and your finger.

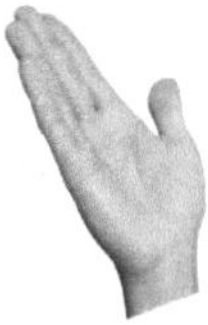

After your Reset breath —

Use your finger & write on your palm.

Write about…

- ✓ What's bothering you.
- ✓ What's replaying in your mind.
- ✓ What you didn't say.

Then close your hand…

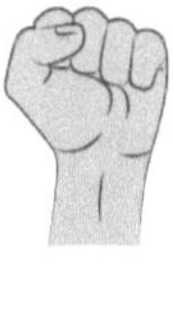

and RELEASE IT by throwing it ***away!***

You can do this…

ANYTIME

ANYWHERE

& NO ONE KNOWS

And the more often you do this…

the more you RELEASE!

> **"Reset. Release.
> Cycle complete."**

I taught this at ***TEDx Princeton.***

Afterward someone came up to tell me they'd *called a friend* in **Germany** during the break — just to tell them about this tool.

Because it works. *Even* in **10** seconds.

Reset. Then release.

Cycle complete.

TRY THIS:

Right now —
before you turn the page.

Think of one thing that has been sitting with you. Something that happened recently that you have not fully released.

Write it on your palm using your finger.

Whatever it is. However messy. However unfinished.

Now crumple it up and throw it away.

Notice how your body feels.

That's the drain opening.

CHAPTER TAKEAWAY:

Writing releases the pressure.
Destroying it closes the cycle.
You do not need paper. You do not need time. You just need 10 seconds and your hand.

Chapter 8:
More Ways to Release

The **Dump N Destroy** is powerful.

But it's not the *only way* to release.

IMPORTANT POINT:

The same tool WON'T work

for ***everyone!***

The key is to find…

The ones that **work** for *you.*

Another IMPORTANT point -

We MUST have

RELEASE tools

that we can use

anytime & anywhere.

The Quick Three to Release

Walk

Movement = RELEASE

You *don't* need a long walk.

You *don't* need a gym.

You just **need to move.**

➔ Walk to the bathroom.

➔ Take the stairs.

➔ Pick your feet up & down under the table if you're sitting.

➔ Tap your foot if you're standing.

Talk

Another **POWERFUL** release is

simply saying it **out loud.**

Just to ***get it out*** of your body

& into the air so it

CAN'T loop in your head anymore.

And if there's nobody around?

Use the **Empty Chair Method**

You start talking to the

"Empty Chair"

As if the person was there!

It's a great way to RELEASE.

Shake

Remember our  ?

After the leopard left — it **shook**

to DISCHARGE every bit of

trapped **survival energy** from its body.

You can do the same thing.

Here's how…

- *Shake* your hands out.
- *Shake* your arms.
- Let your whole-body *tremble* for just a few seconds.

It may feel *silly* **at first.**

DO IT ANYWAY!

Here's the truth —

Any **physical action**

can work as a RELEASE.

Walking, shaking, stretching, jumping.

It's the fact you're MOVING the **energy**

Out of your body

instead of holding it in.

💡 **OVERFLOW INSIGHT:**

The Quick Three are always with you.
No equipment. No time. No excuse.
Walk. Talk. Shake.
That's all it takes to open the drain.

TRY THIS:

From the list above — pick ONE release tool that feels most natural to you right now.

Walk. Talk. Shake. Dump N Destroy. Scribble. Magic Palm Dump.

Just one.

Commit to using it once today. After something hard. After something that sticks with you.

Notice what shifts.

Because that is how this starts. Not with a complete routine. With one tool. Used once. Today.

CHAPTER TAKEAWAY:

*Release looks different for everyone.
Walk it out. Talk it out. Write it out.
The method matters less than the
commitment to actually doing it.*

PART 4:

PROTECT – Keep The Tub From Overflowing

Chapter 8:
More Ways to Release

Has this ***ever***

happened to you?

- You drive home replaying a situation.
- You sit at dinner, but you are not really present.
- You wake up at 2am thinking about a decision you made or something you couldn't prevent.

If you're like *99%* of my clients,

You'll say:

" **YES –** It happens **everyday.** "

Your BODY left **work...**

But your mind is ***still there.***

Here's what that does to your tub.

Every time you…

Replay it — **more** water.

Rethink it — **more** water.

Carry it into your evening — **more** water.

You RESET during the day.

You RELEASED during the day.

But you come home & quietly

refill the tub without even *realizing it.*

💡 **OVERFLOW INSIGHT:**

Your mind does not know how to clock out. Nobody taught it how. And until you give it a clear signal that the day is done — it will keep running.

> **"Your body left.**
> **But your mind stayed."**

There's something IMPORTANT you need to *understand* WHY this happens.

A "YES" *DOESN'T* mean:

→ You're *failing* at self-care.

→ You're *weak.*

→ You're *too emotionally* involved.

A "YES" ***MEANS:***

☑ You're trained to ***care deeply.***

☑ To ***stay vigilant.***

☑ To keep processing until you ***find the answer*** or the solution.

The problem is —

Your brain *doesn't* know how to clock out.

Nobody TAUGHT IT how.

So you try different strategies:

✓ *Once I get on the highway I'll stop thinking about it.*

Still thinking about it.

✓ *Once I cross the bridge I'll leave it all behind.*

Still there. Right next to you.

✓ Once I walk through my front door work stays outside.

And somehow it follows you right through the door. Sits at the dinner table. Climbs into bed.

I **tried** every single one of

those **STRATEGIES.**

And **none** of them worked.

Not one.

Until I found something that did!

TRY THIS:

Tonight — notice what happens when you leave work.

Does stress follow you home?

Does it sit at the dinner table with you?

Does it climb into bed?

Just notice. No judgment. Just awareness.

🗝 CHAPTER TAKEAWAY:

Your brain does not automatically clock out when your body does. Without a clear signal that the day is done — it keeps running. And the tub keeps filling.

Chapter 10:
The Backpack Ritual

I want to *share* how I discovered this.

It did NOT

come from a textbook.

It came from **desperation.**

I was in the thick of my own overflow.

My  would not shut off

at the end of the day.

I'd be home with my family &

mentally still at work.

- *Replaying* cases.
- *Running* through conversations.
- *Worrying* about what I could have done differently.

I tried **EVERYTHING.**

Then 1 day I was walking out of the hospital and I *noticed* something.

A big garbage can.

Right there by the exit door.

Just sitting there.

And something clicked.

I ***imagined*** everything from that day —

Every difficult case.
Every stressful interaction,
Every worry,
Every bit of coworker drama

I *put into* a backpack on my shoulders.

And **before** I walked out the door —

I took off the backpack

& *imagined* ***I THREW IT***

in that garbage can.

Then I *walked out.*

And for the 1st time —

I drove home & WORK didn't follow me.

Not because… I *forced* it out.

or

I distracted myself.

But because my brain had a picture.

A clear *vivid* **IMAGE** of exactly

where that *backpack was.*

In the garbage can.

Back where *I left it.*

Not in the car with me.

💡 **OVERFLOW INSIGHT:**
Your brain does not respond to verbal commands when it is emotionally activated.
But an image?
An image bypasses the thinking brain entirely and speaks directly to the emotional brain.

Here Is Why This Works

Most of the techniques we try to leave work behind are **verbal** or **logical.**

An example:

'I am going to stop thinking about this.'

'Work stays on the other side of that bridge.'

But you CAN'T think your way out of an **emotional state.**

When you picture that backpack

in that garbage can —

your  registers

it as *something real.*

Something that *actually* **happened!**

The truly **powerful** part...

Every time a *work thought*

tries to sneak in - just

picture the backpack in the can.

And the **thought stops!**

The image overrides the thought.

Every single time.

Over time the thoughts get ***quieter.***

Because you've TRAINED your brain

to *leave* **work at work.**

TRY THIS:

Tonight at the end of your day —
try the Backpack Ritual.

Close your eyes. Imagine a backpack on your shoulders. Pack everything from today into it. Every difficult moment. Every worry. Every thought that has been following you.

Imagine a garbage can at the exit door of wherever you work.

Take off the backpack.
Throw it in.
Feel your shoulders drop.
And walk away.

Notice what happens on the drive home.

CHAPTER TAKEAWAY:

Your brain needs a clear picture of where the day ends. The Backpack Ritual gives it one — and once it has that image it stops dragging the day home with you.

Chapter 11:
Protect Yourself Like You Protect Everyone Else

Here's a couple ? 's for you:

1) *Would you run critical equipment without proper maintenance and expect it to keep performing?*

2) *Would you drive a car with no oil and expect the engine to last?*

3) *Would you pour from an empty vessel and expect it to keep filling other people up?*

And yet —

That's exactly what you're *likely*

doing to yourself every single day.

You give. And give. And give some more.

Until there is nothing left.

Then you *wonder*

WHY

you **feel** the way you feel.

OVERFLOW INSIGHT:

Protecting yourself is not selfish.
It's how you stay healthy enough
to keep showing up for
the people who need you.

The Two Things That Keep the Tub From Overflowing

1) Boundaries:

Here's what I've learned in 34 years of working in healthcare.

If you NEVER say **"NO"** —

eventually YOU suffer.

And then… everyone suffers

➔ The people you *serve.*

➔ The people you *love.*

➔ Your *colleagues.*

➔ And ***YOU***

Saying no –

It's NOT abandoning the people who **need** you.

It's HOW you stay **Healthy** enough

to *keep showing up* for them.

The Key to Success:

Start small!

Just identify one boundary this week.

One place where you've been *giving* more

than you can **sustainably** give.

And practice saying no there. Just once.
Just this week.

> **"Saying no is not abandonment.
> It is maintenance."**

2) Self-Care That's Not Optional

<u>I want to ask you something important:</u>

What's 1 thing you could do today —

Just one — that is purely for you?

Not for…

The *people* you serve.

Your *family*.

Your *team*.

For YOU!

A walk

A relaxing bath

Sitting in silence with something you enjoy.

Doing absolutely nothing for 20 minutes.

That's not selfish —

That's CRITICAL maintenance.

Here's the truth:

You DON'T have to **choose** between

being extraordinary at what you do

&

being a healthy human being.

You just need to protect yourself

like you protect everyone else.

With the same consistency.

The same commitment.

The same care.

TRY THIS:

Two things this week.

First — try the Backpack Ritual every day at the end of your workday. Even if it feels strange at first. Do it anyway.

Second — write down ONE boundary you could practice this week. It does not have to be big. But it has to be real.

Protecting yourself is a practice. And it starts with one decision.

Because you cannot change what you cannot see.

CHAPTER TAKEAWAY:

You cannot keep giving what you never restore. Boundaries and self-care are not luxuries — they are the maintenance that keeps you in the work you love.

PART 5:

The Complete System

Chapter 12: The Complete Overflow RESET System™

Let's take a *moment…*

Look at how FAR you've come!

You now **understand** something

MOST people spend their entire lives

never discovering.

That what you've been feeling is not

BURNOUT

Your compartment is overflowing.

And overflowing tubs DON'T

need to be *replaced.*

They need to be **drained.**

**"Reset. Release. Protect.
The Complete Overflow RESET System™"**

Here's your **complete** system in one place.

THE TUB

The tub is **YOU.**

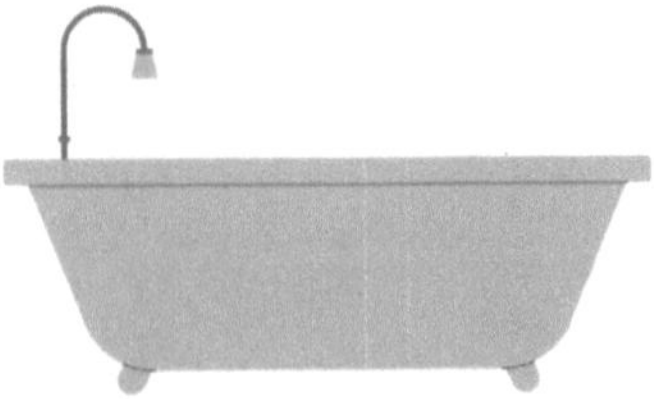

Everything that goes into your day

⇩

is water *running* from the faucet.

When the faucet NEVER **turns off**

& the drain ***stays closed*** —

you OVERFLOW.

That overflow is what you've been calling

BURNOUT

But it's **NOT** burnout.

It's an *overflowing* tub.

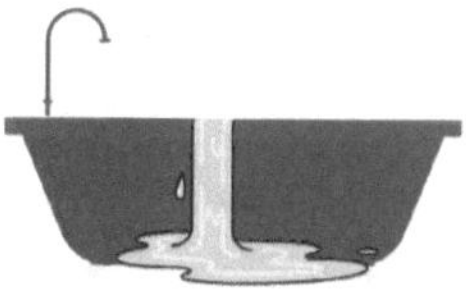

And overflowing tubs have a

SOLUTION!

STEP 1: RESET — Turn Off the Faucet

When you feel your

stress faucet **turn on…**

PAUSE

Do 3 RESET breaths:

Breathe IN:
(thru the nose)

S L O W
count of 5

Breathe OUT:
(thru the mouth)

S L O W
count of 5

10 seconds. *Anywhere. Anytime.*

The faucet turns off.

STEP 2: RELEASE — Open the Drain

After you RESET — RELEASE

- ✓ Walk it out. 
- ✓ Talk it out.
- ✓ Shake it out. 
- ✓ Dump N Destroy
- ✓ The Magic Palm Dump

Physical action that moves the stress energy OUT of your body.

Movement = RELEASE

The **drain** opens. Your level GOES down!

STEP 3: PROTECT — Keep the Tub From Overflowing Again

1) At the end of *every* workday —

do the **Backpack Ritual.**

Your work STAYS where you left it.

You come home.

2) Practice **saying "NO"** when your body is *telling you* it needs rest.

3) Do 1 thing every single day that's **PURELY for you.**

💡 **OVERFLOW INSIGHT:**

Reset turns off the faucet.
Release opens the drain.
Protect keeps it from overflowing again.
Three steps. Done together. Every day.

"This is not something you finish.
It is something you use."

Why This Works When Nothing Else Has

Most stress management programs give you 1 step.

Calm down.

Breathe.

Take a walk.

Those things matter.

They **turn off** the faucet.

But they leave the tub full.

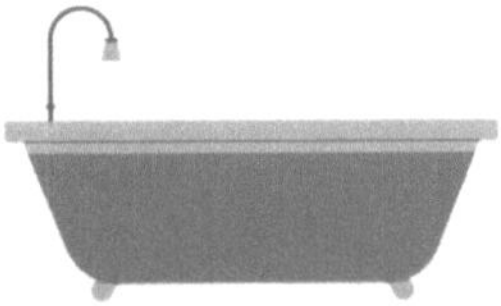

The **Overflow RESET System™** is different because it addresses all

3 parts of the problem.

Those are:

1) A **stress response** designed to *keep activating.*

2) The **accumulated stress** that *keeps building.*

3) The habits & rituals that keep the tub from refilling unnecessarily.

We'll 

what *shows* up in our life.

However…

This system *gives* *YOU* *back* **control**

so life's NOT controlling you!

Use it when you ***need*** it the MOST…

Right now. In real time.

TRY THIS:

Today — use all 3 steps in sequence The next time you feel the stress response activate:

Reset — three rounds of 5-count breathing.

Release — walk, talk, shake or Dump N Destroy.

Protect — at the end of your day, do the Backpack Ritual.

Notice what is different.

This is not theory. This is your nervous system doing exactly what it was designed to do — when you finally give it the right tools.

CHAPTER TAKEAWAY:

Reset turns off the faucet. Release opens the drain. Protect keeps it from overflowing again. Three steps. Done together. In real time. Every day.

Chapter 13: Your Passion Doesn't Have to Destroy You

I want to *close* with something I **mean** with everything I have.

What you do matters profoundly.

Whether you're…

- *Keeping* people alive.
- *Keeping* them safe.
- *Teaching* the next generation.
- *Holding space* for people in crisis.
- *Running toward* what everyone else runs from.

You show up when it's ***hard.***

When it's ***heartbreaking.***

When most people ***could not.***

That takes something extraordinary.

But you ***cannot*** sustain

extraordinary

output from an *empty vessel.*

You ***cannot*** keep giving what you've

never been taught to restore.

> **"Your passion for your work doesn't have to destroy you. It can actually sustain you — when you have the right system."**

Remember…

that bottle of root beer?

The one I **knocked over** in

my car all *those years ago?*

Here's what that bottle taught me

that 30 years in *healthcare* **hadn't:**

It's not about having 

pressure.

That's **NOT** realistic.

Who wants FLAT root beer?

It is about knowing how to RELEASE the **pressure** before it **controls** you.

Because when *you do that* —
you don't just become healthier.

You become even ***better*** at what you do.

- ✓ A *better* professional.
- ✓ A *better* partner.
- ✓ A *better* parent.
- ✓ A *better* human.

Your **passion** for your work does

NOT have to *destroy* you.

It can actually sustain you

When you have the ***RIGHT*** system.

And now — you have it.

💡 OVERFLOW INSIGHT:

You were never meant to carry everything you have been carrying. Not because you are not strong enough. But because your system was never designed to hold it all. It was designed to process it. To release it. To reset.

One Last Thing

You are *going to* have <u>hard</u> days.

➔ Days when the faucet ***runs fast***

and the drain ***feels stuck.*** 

➔ Days when the backpack feels

too heavy to put down.

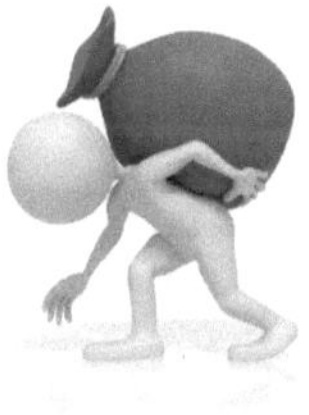

➔ Days when you *wonder* if

any of this is

making a difference.

On *those days* I want you

to **REMEMBER** something.

You're NOT **burned out.**

You're **OVERFLOWING**

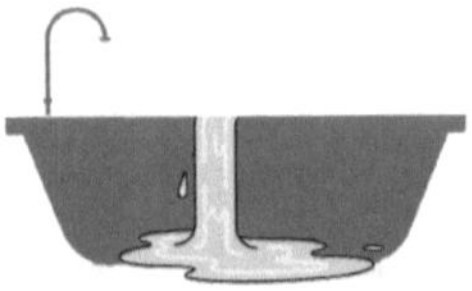

And…

You *now* ***know exactly***

WHAT to do about it.

Reset.

Release.

Protect.

TRY THIS:

Go back to the first 'Try This' in this book. The one that asked you to rate how full your tub was on a scale of 1-10.

Write that number down again — right now.

Then ask yourself:

"What is one thing I am going to do differently starting today?"

Just one thing.

Because that is how this starts.

And that is how it builds.

FINAL TAKEAWAY:

You do not have to choose between being extraordinary at what you do and being a healthy human being. That is a false choice. And it always has been.

WHAT'S NEXT

Going Deeper

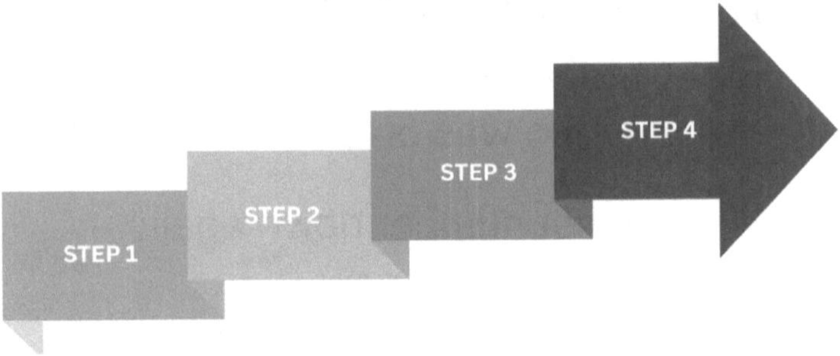

This book gave you the **foundation.**

But *knowing* the system and having it

<u>become automatic</u> in your daily life

are two very different things.

If you want to go deeper — here's how:

STEP 1: The Overflow Check-In Quiz

Free — takes 1 minute

Discover your personal Stress Quotient & see exactly what your tub level is right now.

StressSmarter.info/Check

STEP 2: The 5-Day Overflow RESET Experience

Free — 10 minutes a day

5 days of guided training that walks you thru the complete Overflow RESET System™ — one tool at a time. Perfect for people who want to ***practice*** *what they just read.*

StressSmarter.info/5

STEP 3: The 21-Day Overflow RESET

The complete transformation program

21 days of deep-dive training, personal assignments ***& live coaching*** *— designed to install the Overflow RESET System™ so deeply into your daily life it becomes automatic.*

Includes Carol's ***Frame It™ Guarantee*** *— if your stress doesn't cut in half in 21 days Carol will personally work with you until it does.*

StressSmarter.info/21

STEP 4: The RESET Room™

Monthly live training and coaching

For people who are serious about building the skills, tools and mindset for lasting wellbeing — one month at a time.

Live monthly training. Live monthly coaching. Carol. In real time. Every month.

StressSmarter.info/Reset

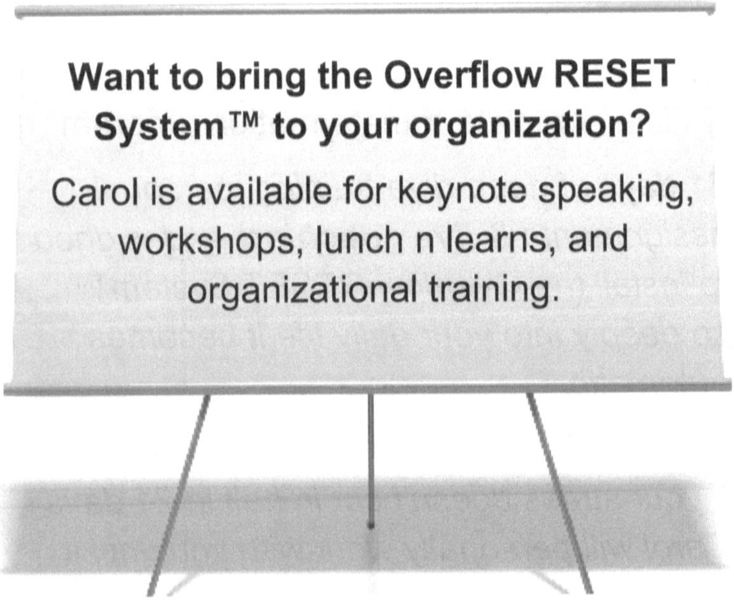

Carol@StressSmarter.zone

StressSmarter.zone

Thank you

*"Thank you for spending this time with me.
What you do matters. And so do you."*

— Carol Rickard, LCSW

2x TEDx Speaker | Healthcare Burnout Expert
Creator of the Overflow RESET System™

About Carol

Carol Rickard, LCSW is a licensed clinical social worker, 2x TEDx speaker, Healthcare Burnout Expert and creator of the Overflow RESET System™ — a simple science-backed two-step method that helps high-performing professionals reset and release stress in real time.

With 34 years of experience in behavioral healthcare Carol has helped thousands of nurses, first responders, teachers, social workers and executives break free from the cycle of accumulated stress and burnout — not by doing more, but by finally learning how to release what they carry.

Her TEDx talk *"Why Stress Never Goes Away (And How to Finally Release It)"* introduced audiences around the world to a completely new way of thinking about stress — including the Magic Palm Dump technique that spread all the way to Germany during a single break at TEDx Princeton.

Carol knows what it takes to manage stress under the most demanding circumstances — because she has lived it. She nearly lost her dream career to stress-induced migraines. She battled undiagnosed depression for two years. And she discovered the two-step system that saved her career — not in a textbook, but in the front seat of her car with a bottle of root beer.

That discovery became the Overflow RESET System™. And it has since changed the lives of thousands of professionals who were told they were burned out — when what they actually were was overflowing.

Carol's work has been trusted by Penn Medicine, Princeton Health, Robert Wood Johnson Foundation, NJ State Police, Philadelphia International Airport, SEPTA and Catholic Charities Diocese of Trenton. Her experise has been featured in Reader's Digest, Woman's World and on the Dr. Oz Show.

She is the author of 30+ books and the creator of a complete Overflow RESET ecosystem — including the free 5-Day Overflow RESET Experience, the 21-Day Overflow RESET Experience and The RESET Room™ — a monthly live training and coaching community for professionals who are serious about thriving, not just surviving.

Carol lives in New Jersey and is available for keynote speaking, corporate training and organizational workshops.

Carol@StressSmarter.zone

StressSmarter.zone

Connect with Carol on:

Linkedin.com/in/CarolRickard

Facebook.com/CarolRickardOfficial

Need More Tools?!

Are you overwhelmed by life these days? The 2 Bucket Rule will give you the secret to finally have lasting peace of mind!

And Carol has written more "tool" books!

If you need help:

- ✓ Losing weight
- ✓ Dealing with anger
- ✓ Managing health issues
- ✓ Beginning meditation
- ✓ Practicing self-care

Take a look at the next few pages…

Self-care is often forgotten in this busy world. Carol offers simple and practical strategies to fit into your busy life!

What if you could take control of stress & anxiety in seconds? Carol shows you EXACTLY how you can do that!

Has your life been touched by cancer? Carol shares the exact steps she used to manage her anxiety during her own cancer.

Available: amazon.com/author/carolrickard

Chronic illness doesn't exclude you from having wellness. Get a blueprint to follow for taking back control of your health!

Are you sick & tired of feeling sick & tired? This is a step-by-step system for reclaiming your life from depression.

Don't let work stress follow you home or impact your wellness. Get a toolbox and take back control of your life!

Available: amazon.com/author/carolrickard

ANGER - one of the most powerful emotions there is. Learn how to manage it instead of it managing you!

Losing weight doesn't have to be complicated! Learn the *7 Laws of Lasting Weight Loss* a car can teach us. Guaranteed to work!

Your mind *is not* supposed to be quiet! Learn how mediation really works & change your life forever!

Do you find yourself struggling with what to say or how to help someone you care about? Learn how to say it & what to

Available: amazon.com/author/carolrickard

WordTools

What are words tools?
They are acronyms with purpose & meaning!

They are officially called *Artinyms*™, which is Sanskrit for "describe".

On the back of each wordtool is a question for you to answer should you choose to!

We have **4 different versions:**

Wellness Vol. 1 & 2, ***Self-Esteem*** Vol. 1 & 2
Business Vol. 1 & 2, ***Athletes*** Vol. 1

Examples:

The
Only
Day
Afforded
You!

A
Deliberate
Adjustment
Providing
Transformation

Daringly
Recognize
Experiences
As
Mine

NEW RELEASE!!!!
Kid these days have to deal with so much stress. This makes sure they have the tools to succeed!!

We have three different versions of adult stress books because life circumstances can be different for each.

Choose the one that ***best fits*** your situation!

Caregiver

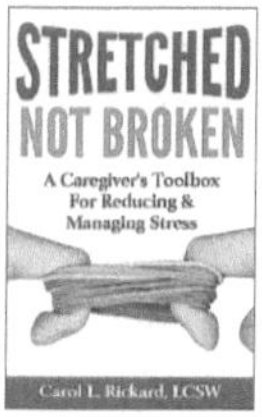

Research has shown caregivers are the MOST vulnerable. Learn quick, simple, practical tools for reducing and managing it.

Stress Eater

Do you find yourself eating when under stress? Get the tools & knowledge needed to break away from any old habits.

General

STRESS… It's all around us and NOT getting any less! Get the system Carol has taught to 1,000's & finally take control!